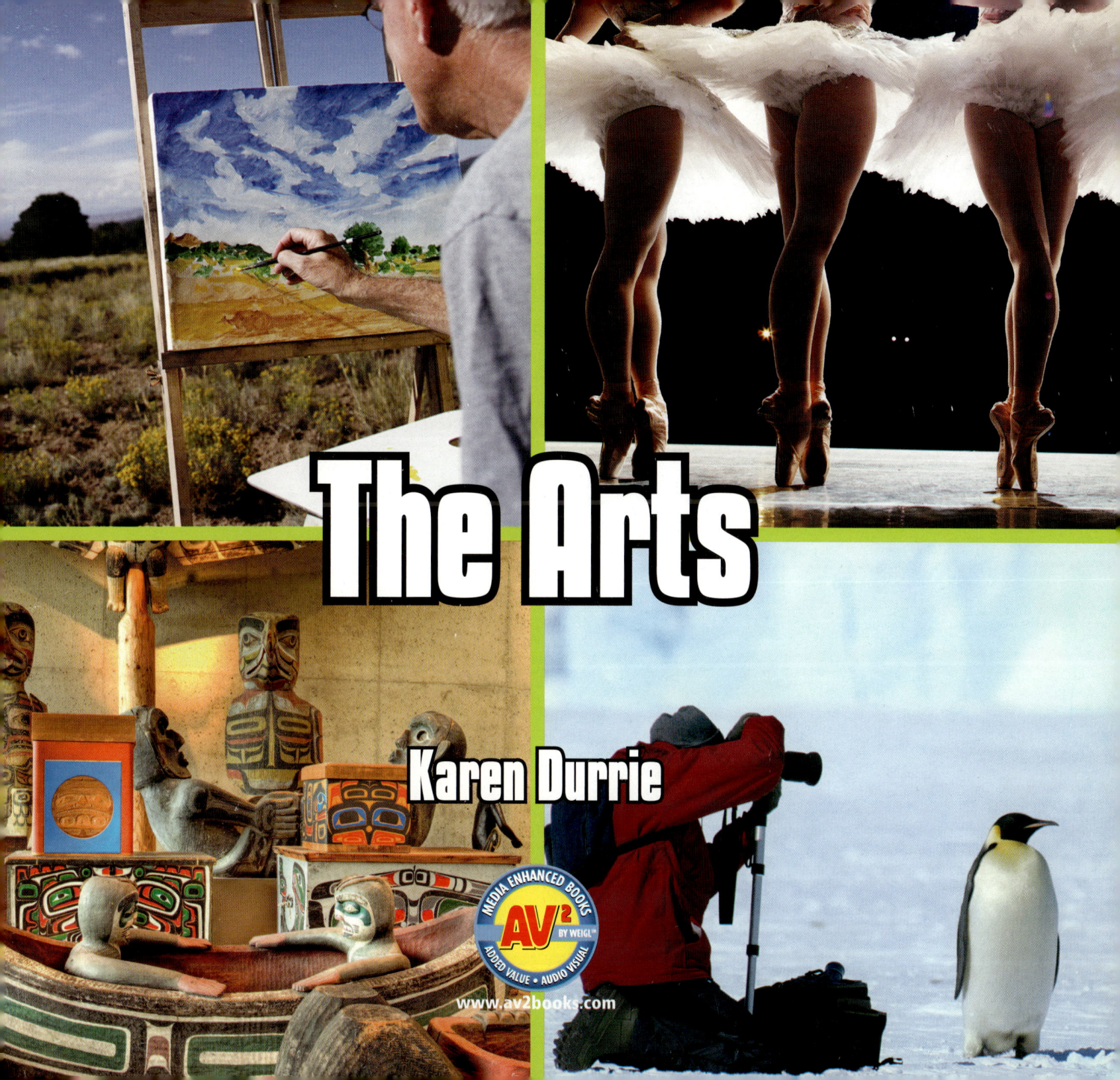
The Arts
Karen Durrie

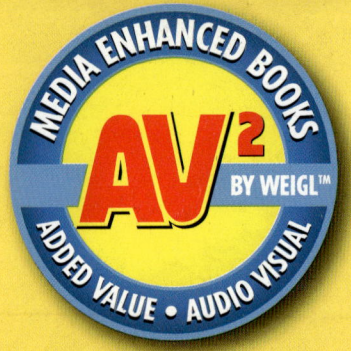

Go to www.av2books.com, and enter this book's unique code.

BOOK CODE

L875856

AV² by Weigl brings you media enhanced books that support active learning.

AV² provides enriched content that supplements and complements this book. Weigl's AV² books strive to create inspired learning and engage young minds in a total learning experience.

Your AV² Media Enhanced books come alive with...

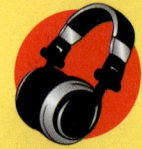
Audio
Listen to sections of the book read aloud.

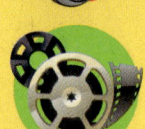
Video
Watch informative video clips.

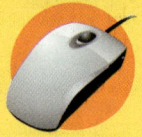
Embedded Weblinks
Gain additional information for research.

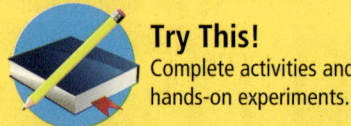
Try This!
Complete activities and hands-on experiments.

Key Words
Study vocabulary, and complete a matching word activity.

Quizzes
Test your knowledge.

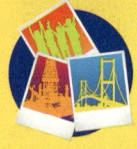
Slide Show
View images and captions, and prepare a presentation.

... and much, much more!

Published by AV² by Weigl
350 5th Avenue, 59th Floor New York, NY 10118
Website: www.av2books.com   www.weigl.com

Copyright ©2012 AV² by Weigl
All rights reserved. No part of this publication may be reproduced, stored in a retrieval system, or transmitted in any form or by any means, electronic, mechanical, photocopying, recording, or otherwise, without the prior written permission of the publisher.

Library of Congress Cataloging-in-Publication Data

Durrie, Karen.
 The arts / Karen Durrie.
   p. cm. -- (Community helpers)
  ISBN 978-1-61690-948-2 (hardcover : alk. paper) -- ISBN 978-1-61690-593-4 (online)
 1. Arts--Juvenile literature. I. Title.
 NX633.D87 2011
  700--dc23
                              201102490

Printed in the United States of America in North Mankato, Minnesota
1 2 3 4 5 6 7 8 9 0 15 14 13 12 11

062011
WEP030611

Project Coordinator: Karen Durrie Art Director: Terry Paulhus

Weigl acknowledges Getty Images as the primary image supplier for this title.

The Arts

CONTENTS

- 2 AV² Book Code
- 4 What Are the Arts?
- 6 Artist
- 8 Filmmaker
- 10 Curator
- 12 Actor
- 14 Writer
- 16 Dancer
- 18 Musician
- 20 Photographer
- 22 Arts Facts
- 24 Word List

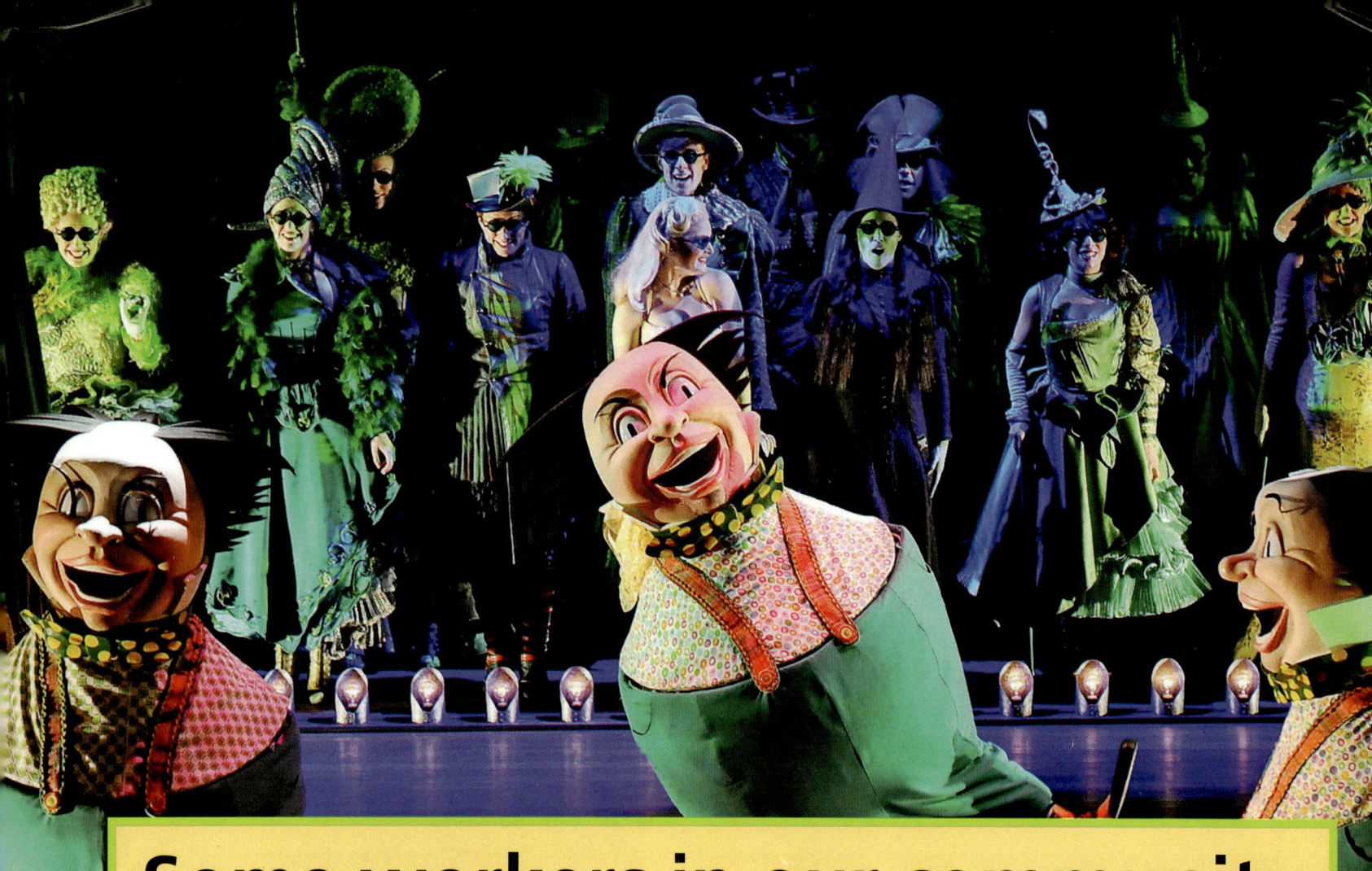

Some workers in our community tell stories through art, dance, writing, and music.

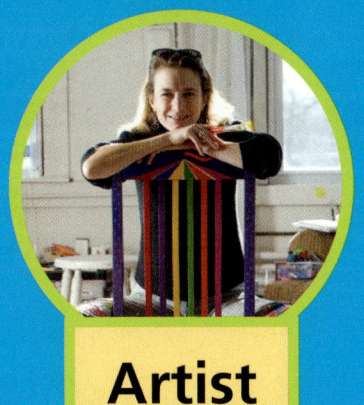 **Artist**

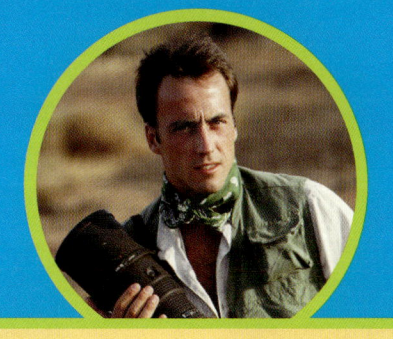 **Photographer**

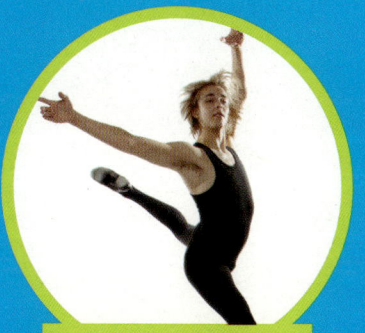 **Dancer**

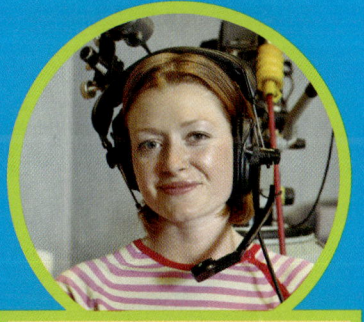 **Filmmaker**

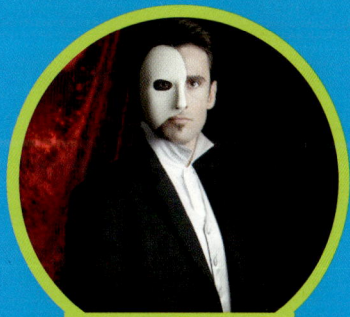 **Actor**

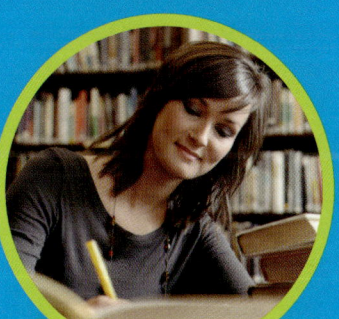 **Writer**

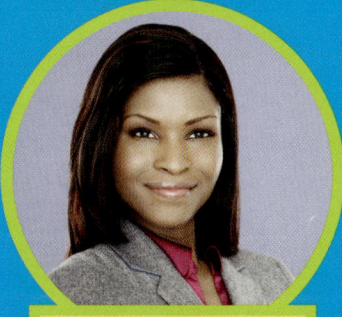 **Curator**

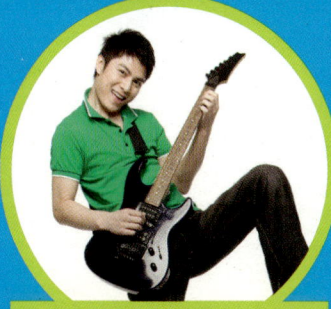 **Musician**

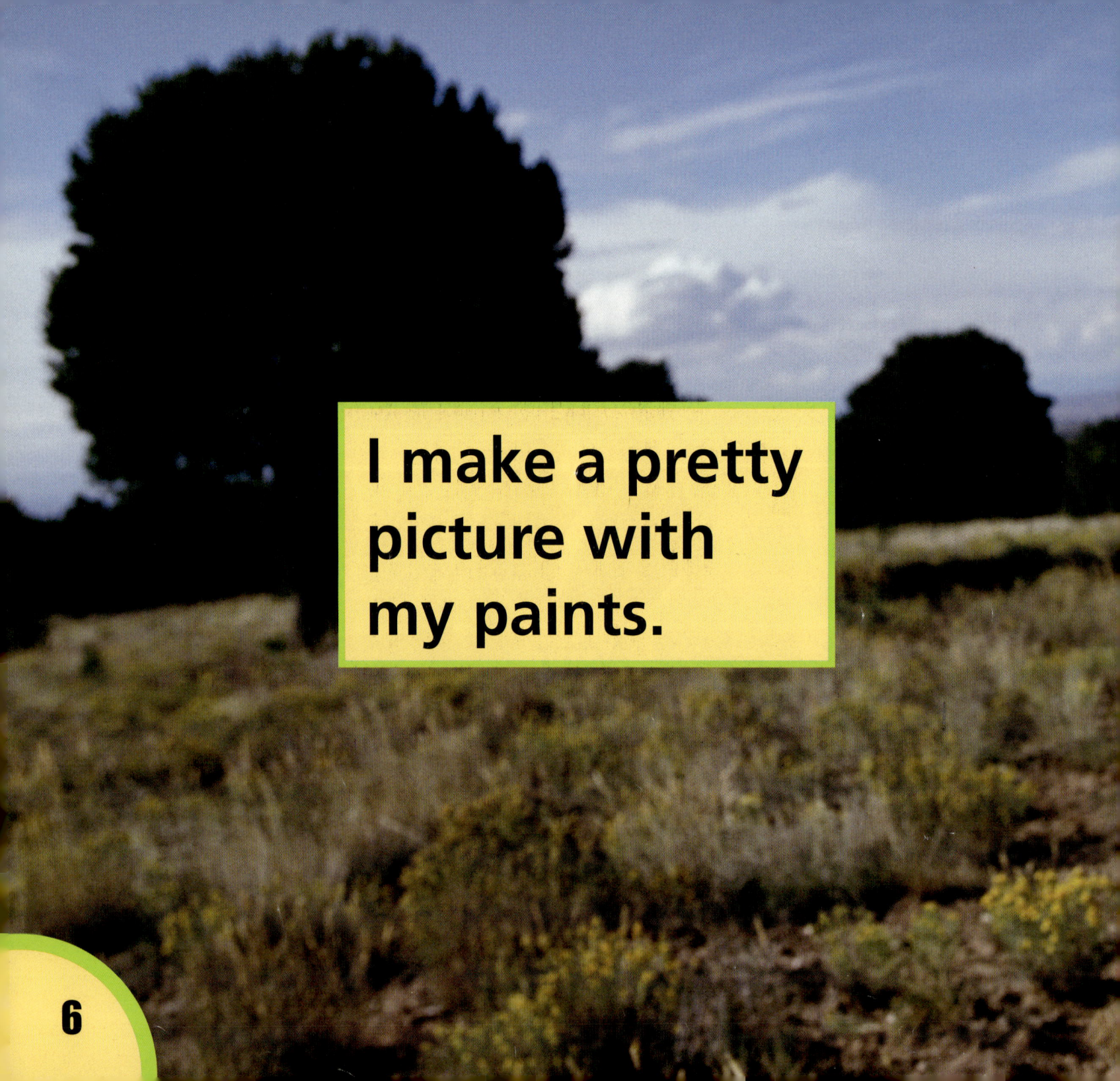

I make a pretty picture with my paints.

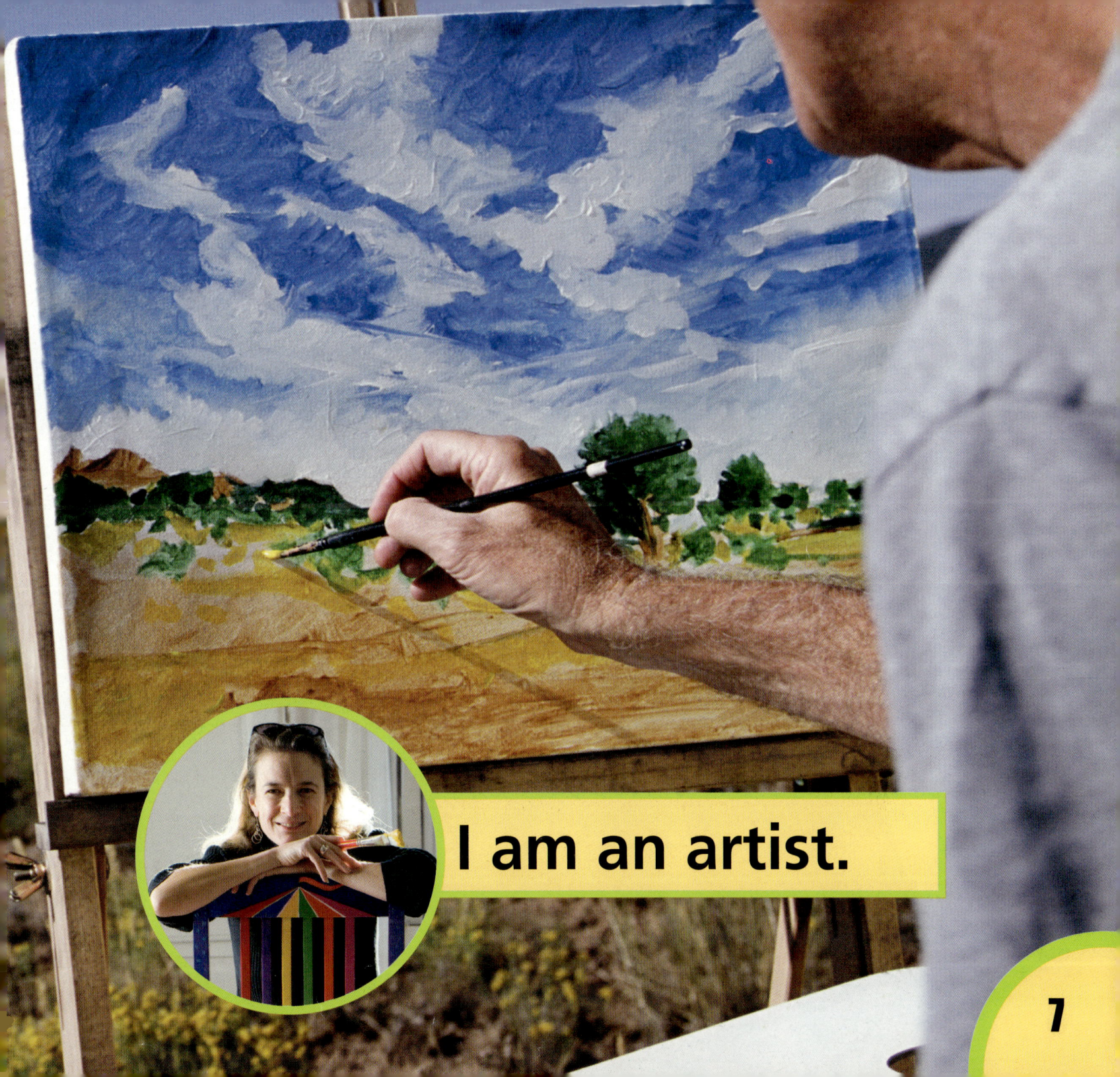

I am an artist.

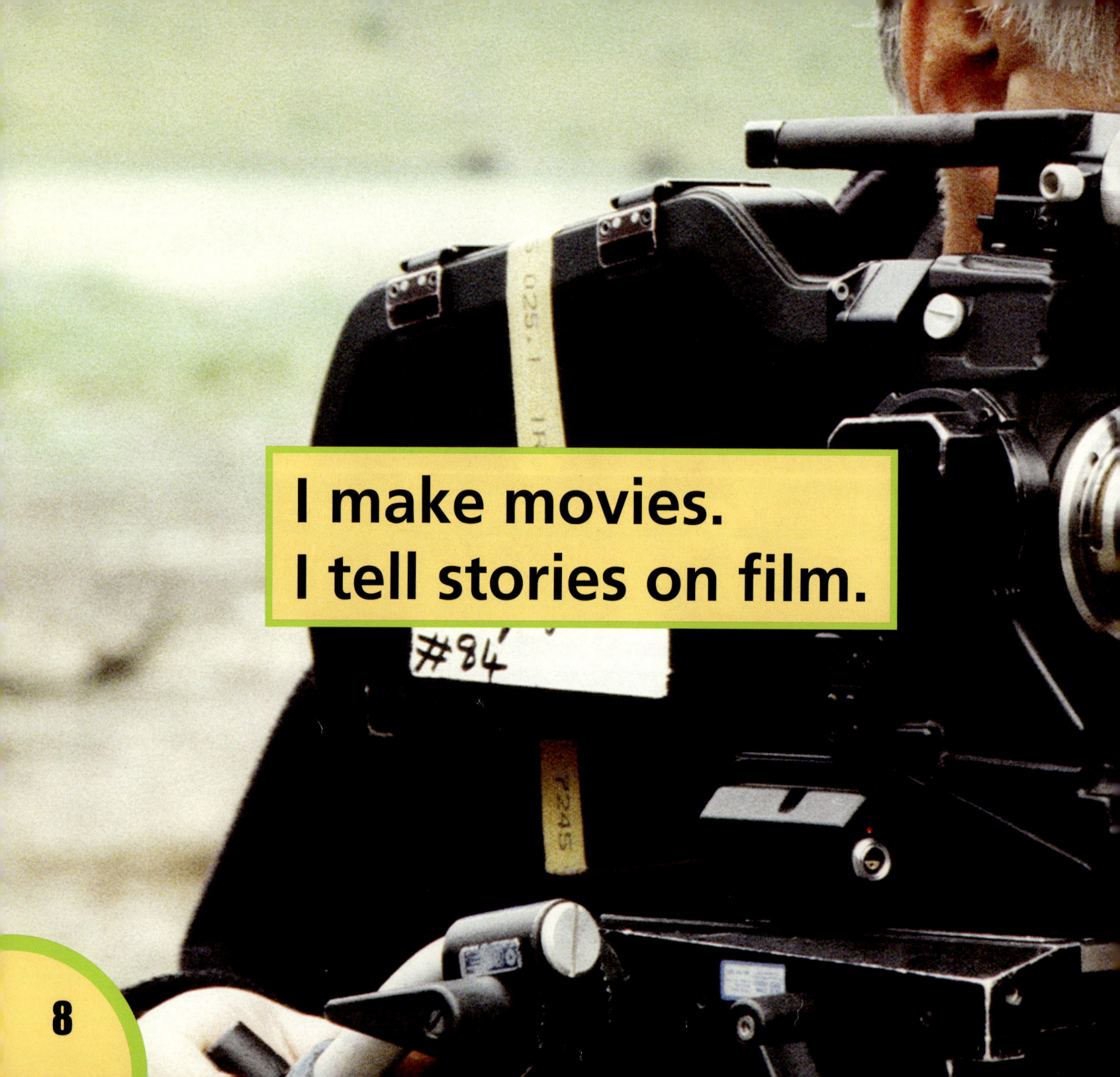
I make movies.
I tell stories on film.

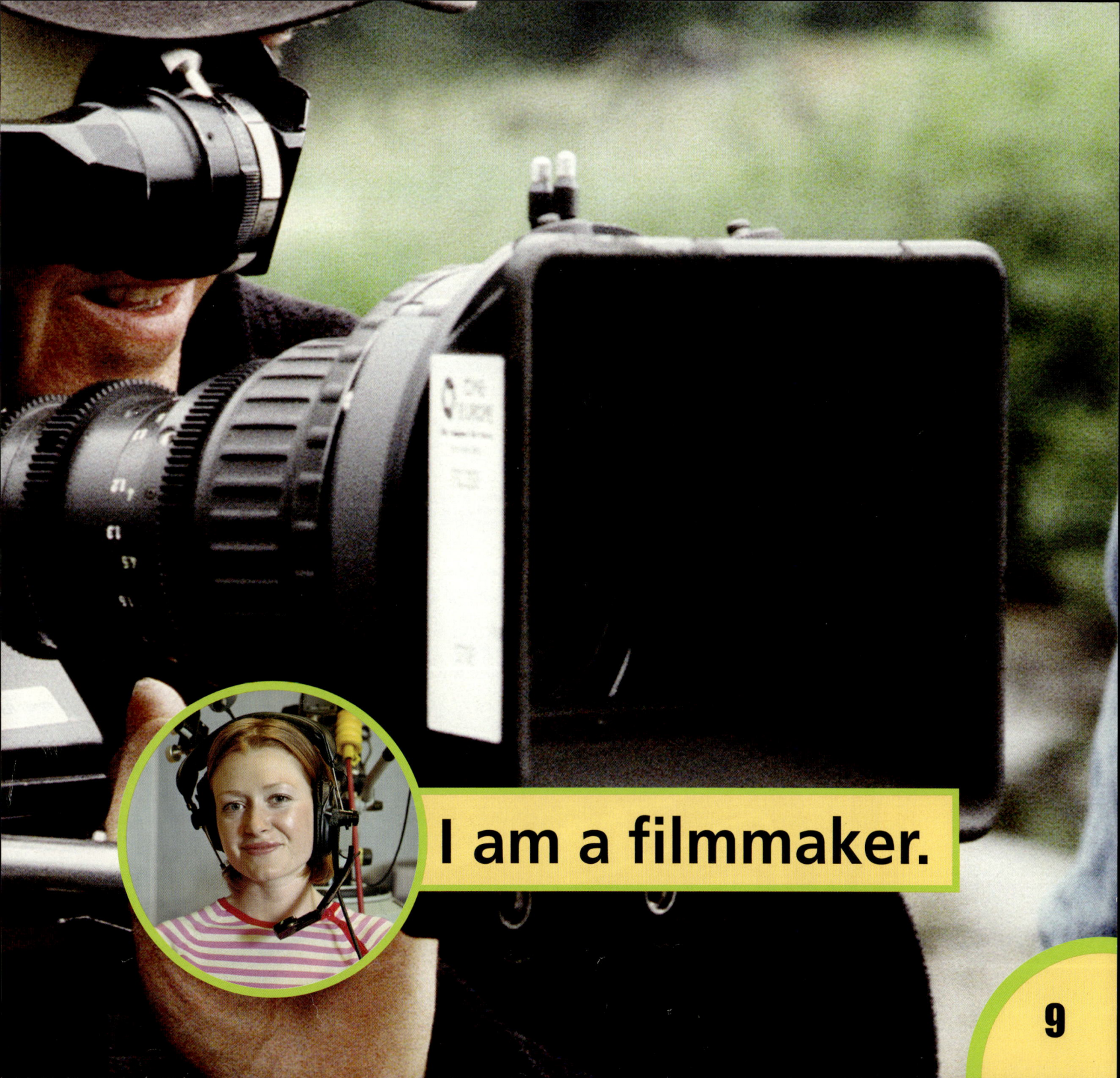

I am a filmmaker.

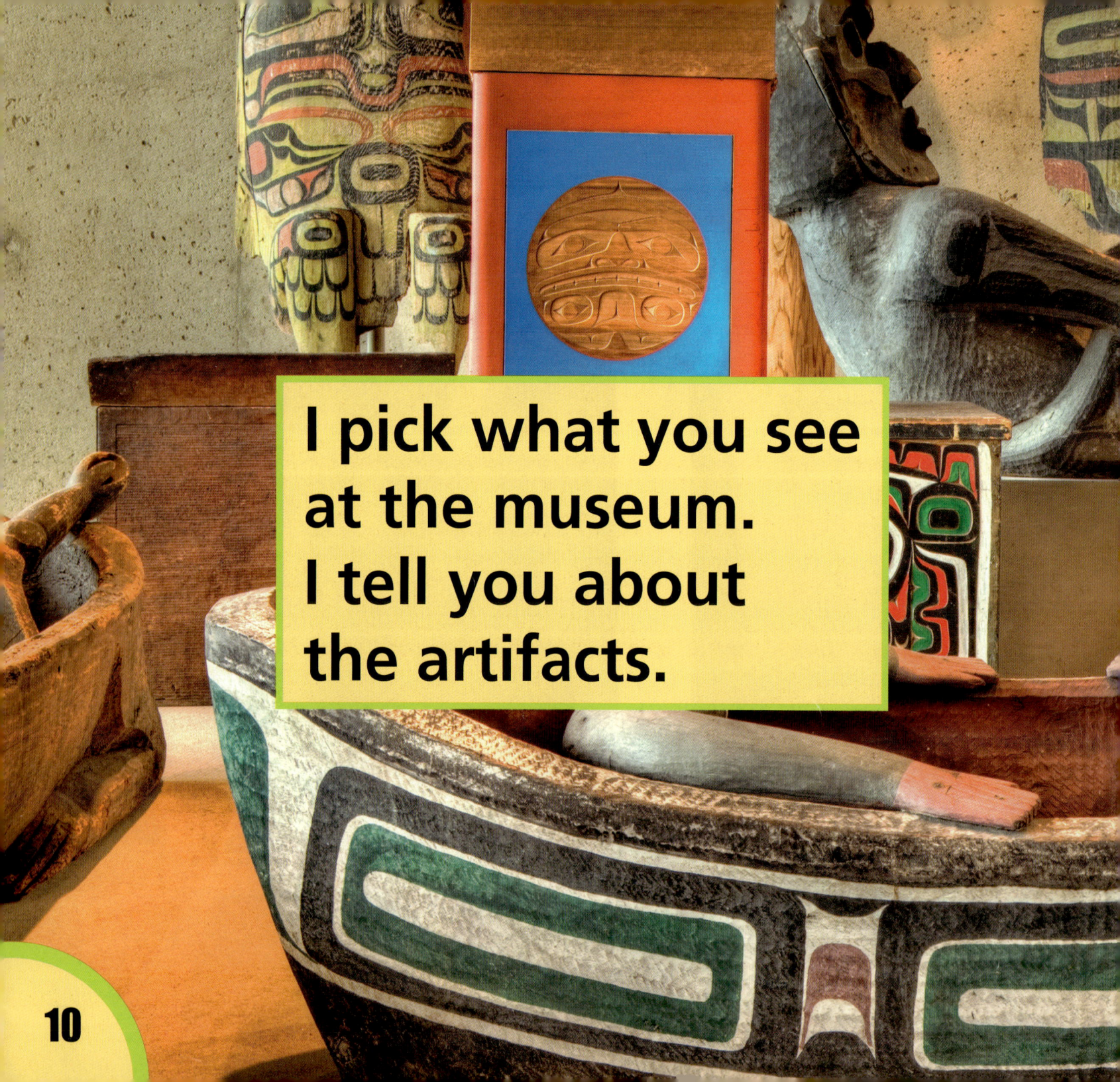

I pick what you see at the museum. I tell you about the artifacts.

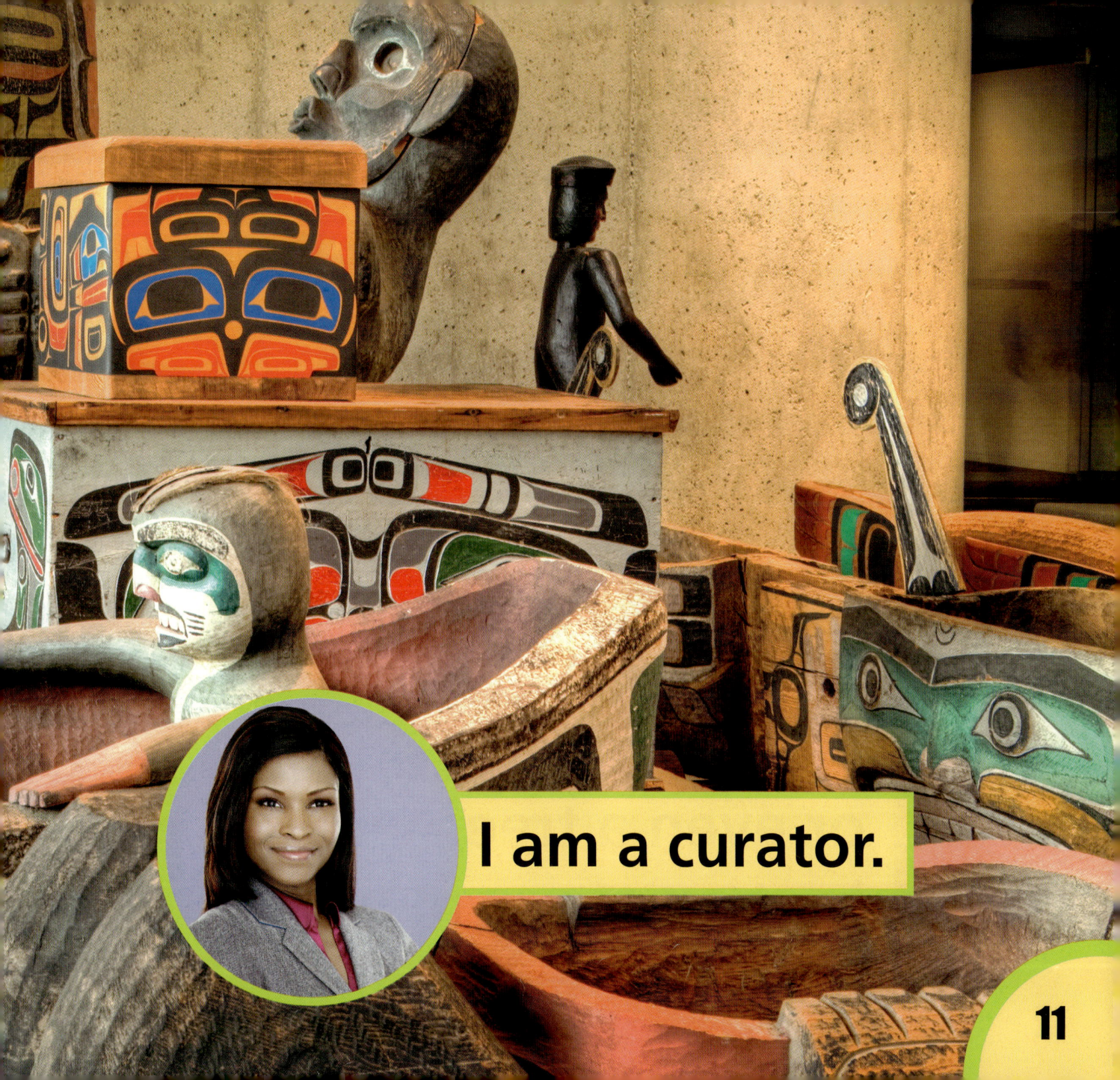

I am a curator.

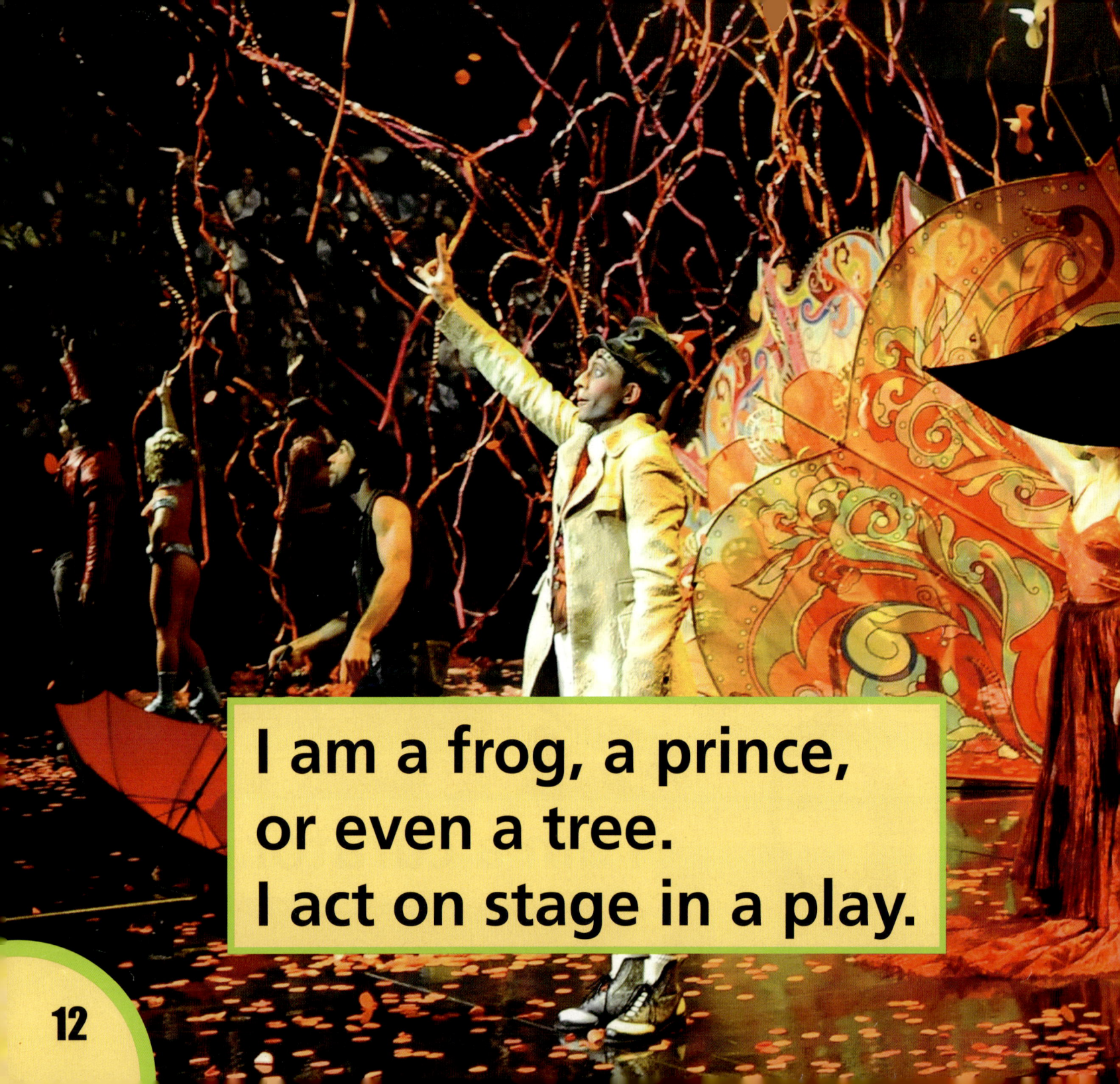

I am a frog, a prince, or even a tree.
I act on stage in a play.

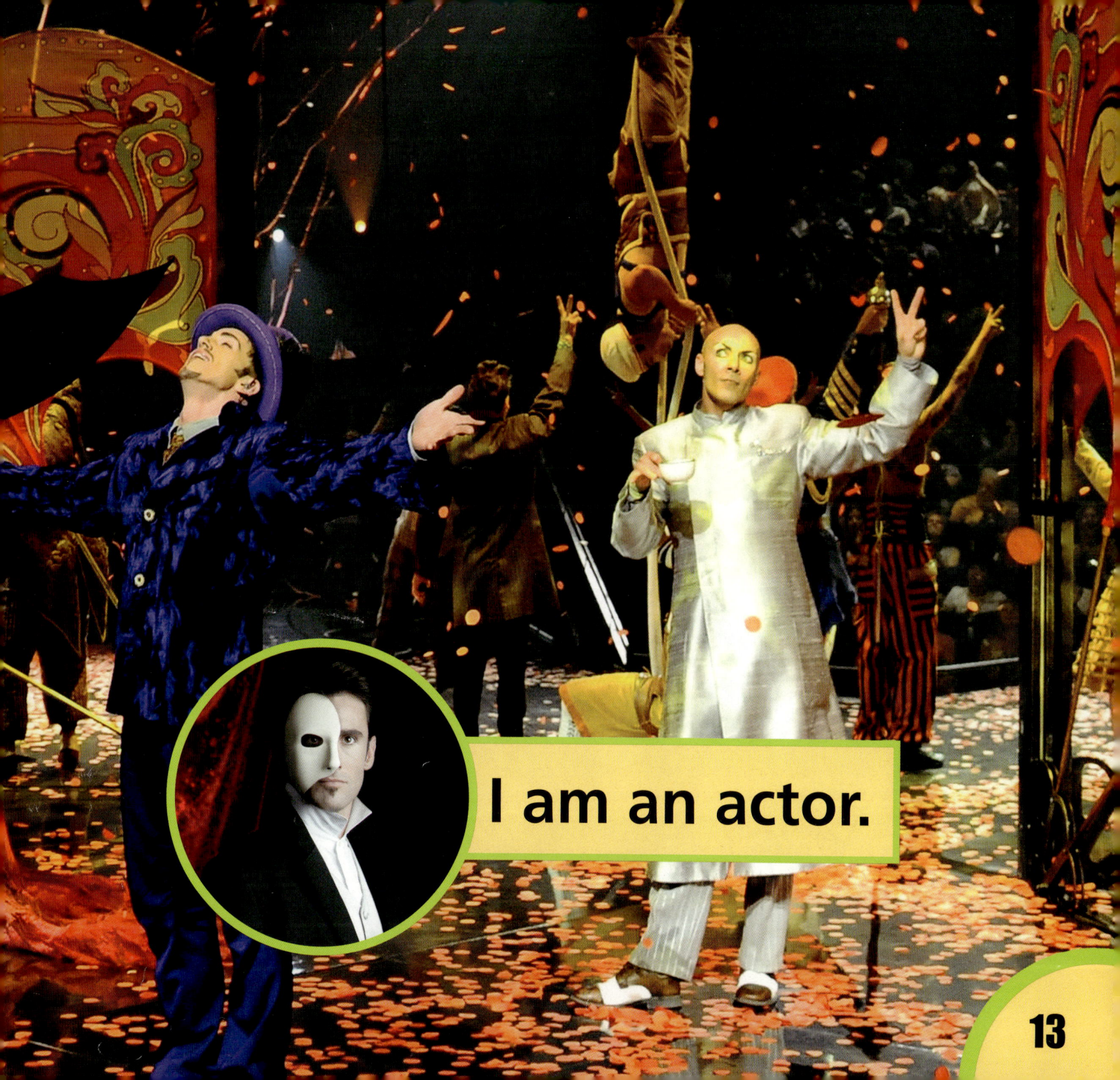

I am an actor.

13

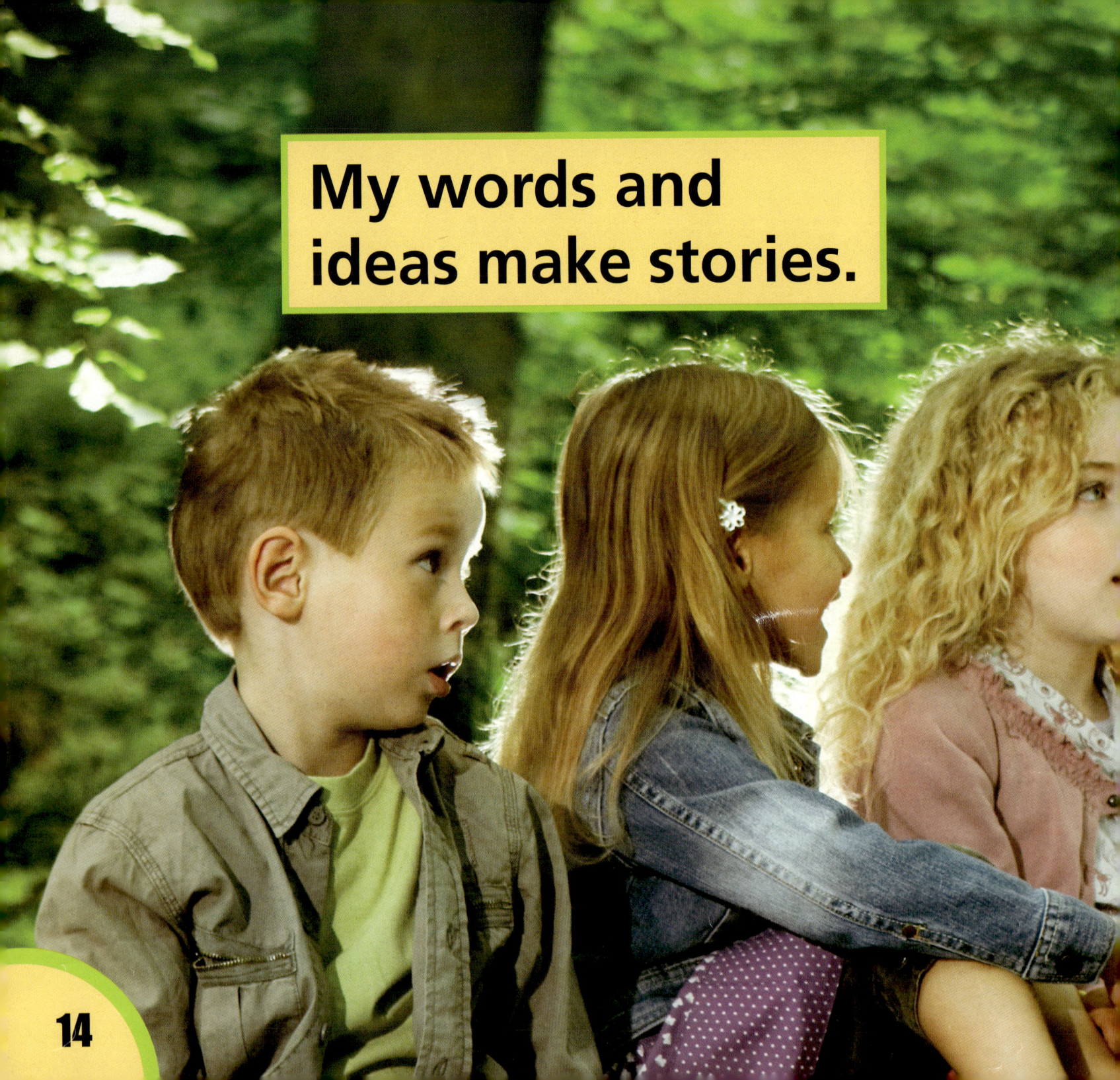
My words and ideas make stories.

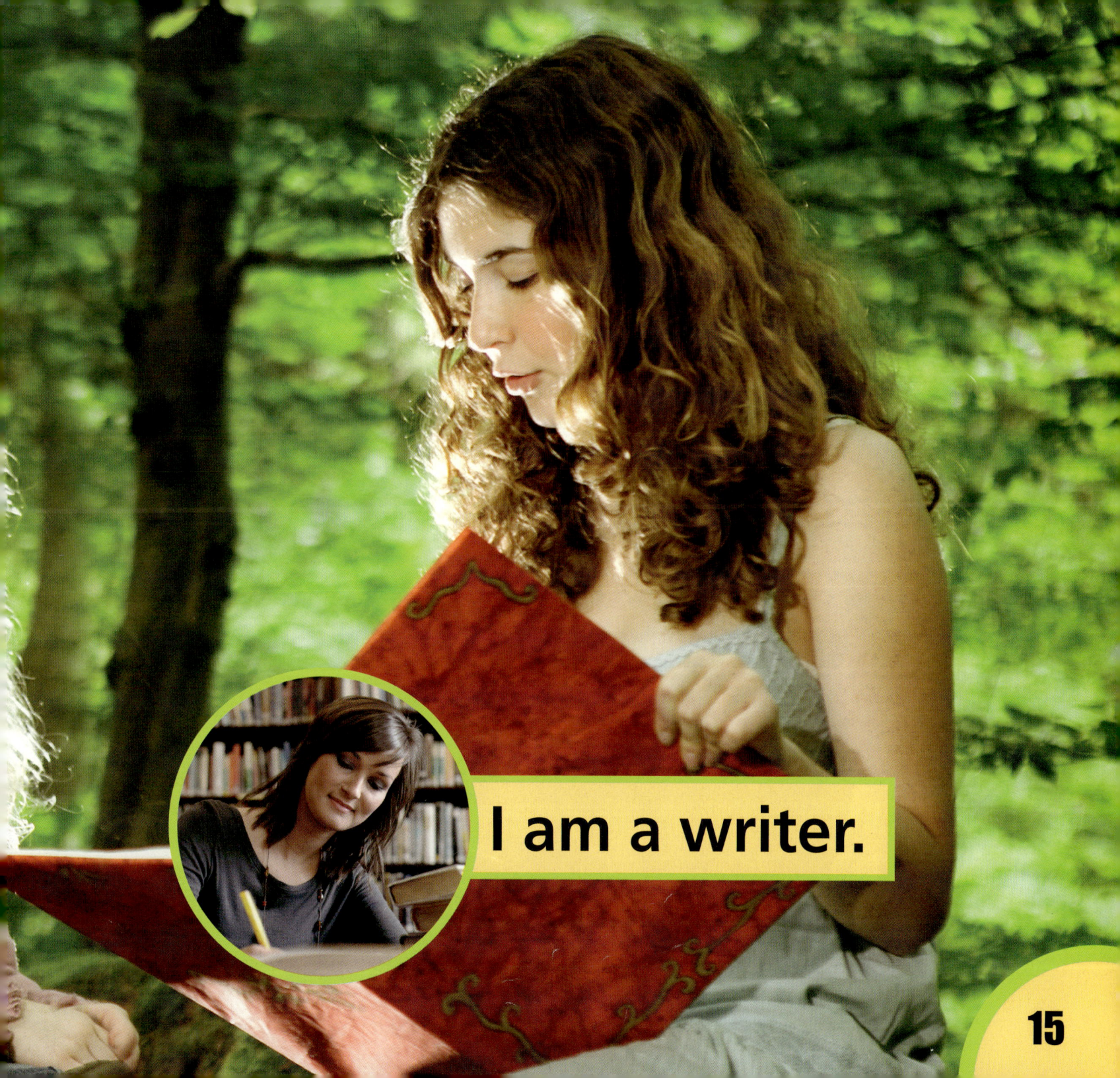

I am a writer.

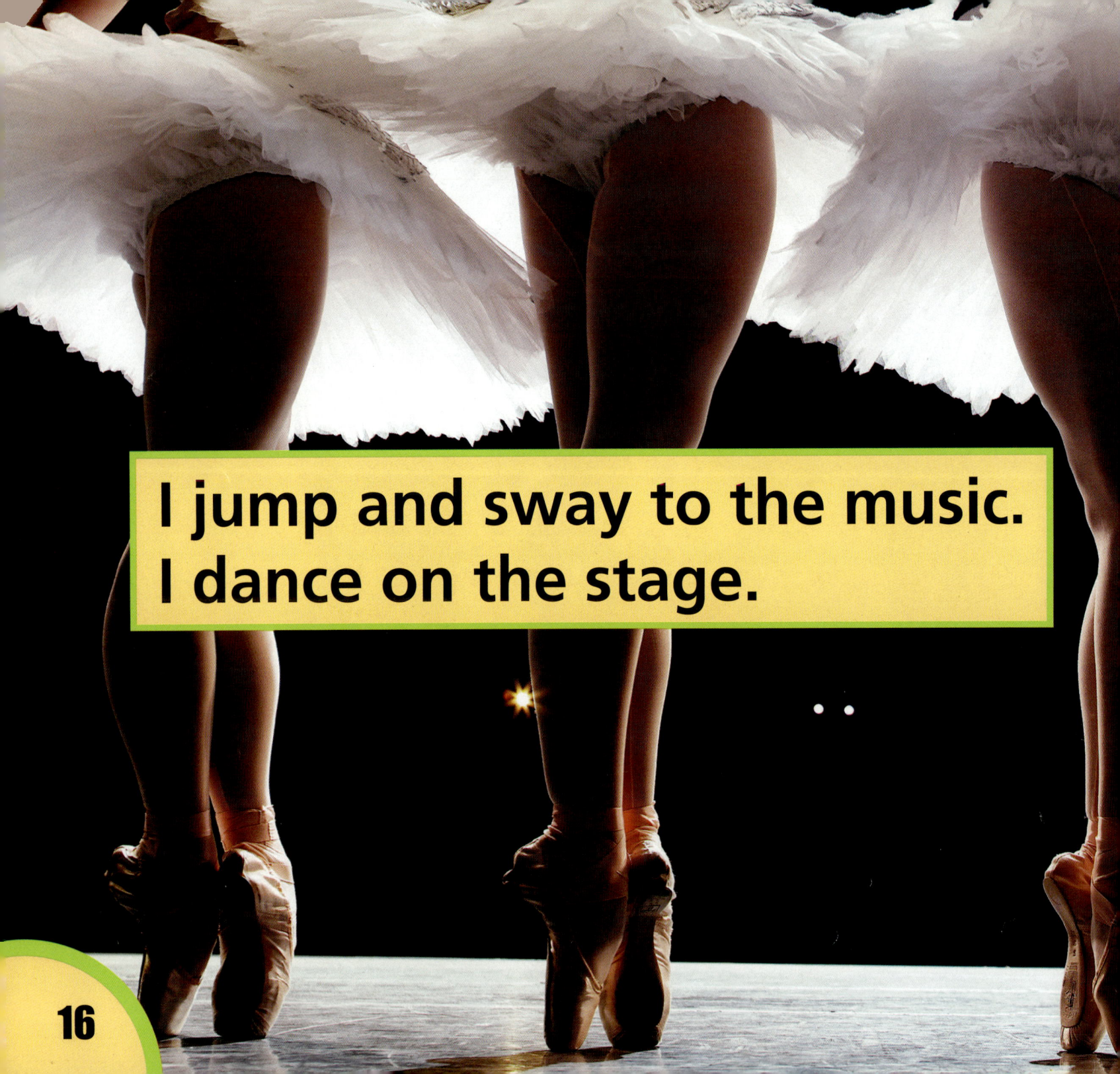

I jump and sway to the music.
I dance on the stage.

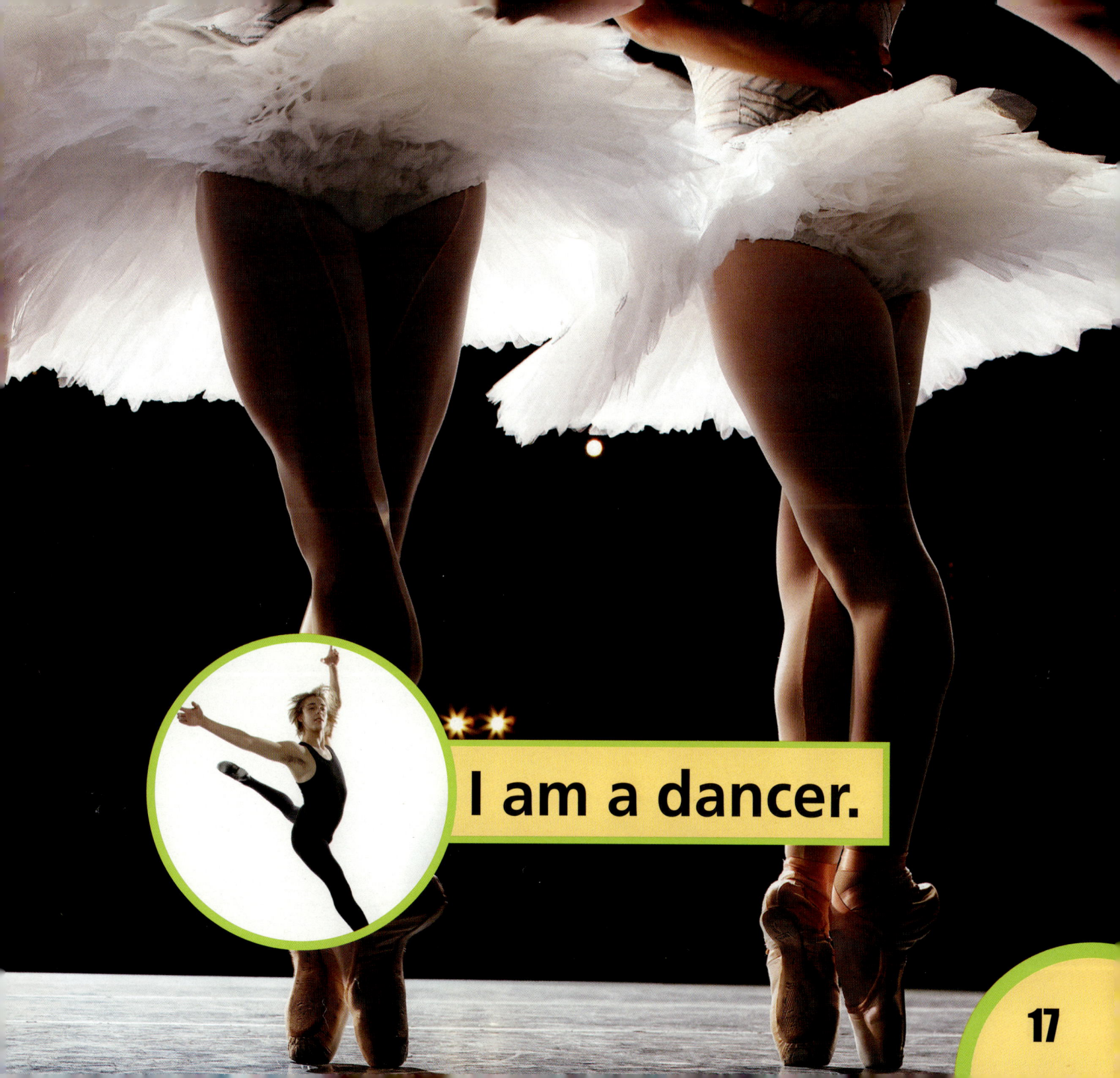

I am a dancer.

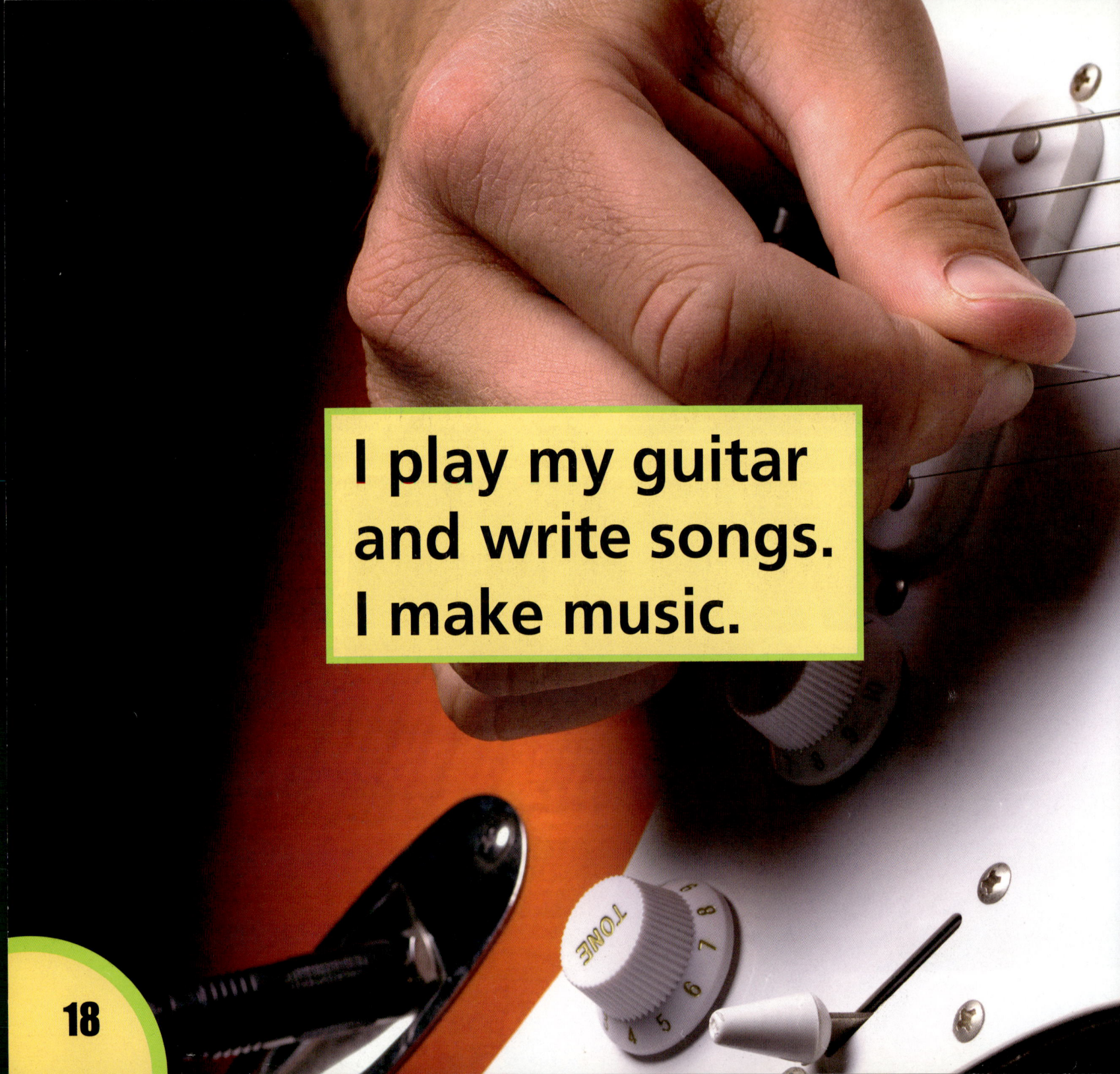

I play my guitar and write songs. I make music.

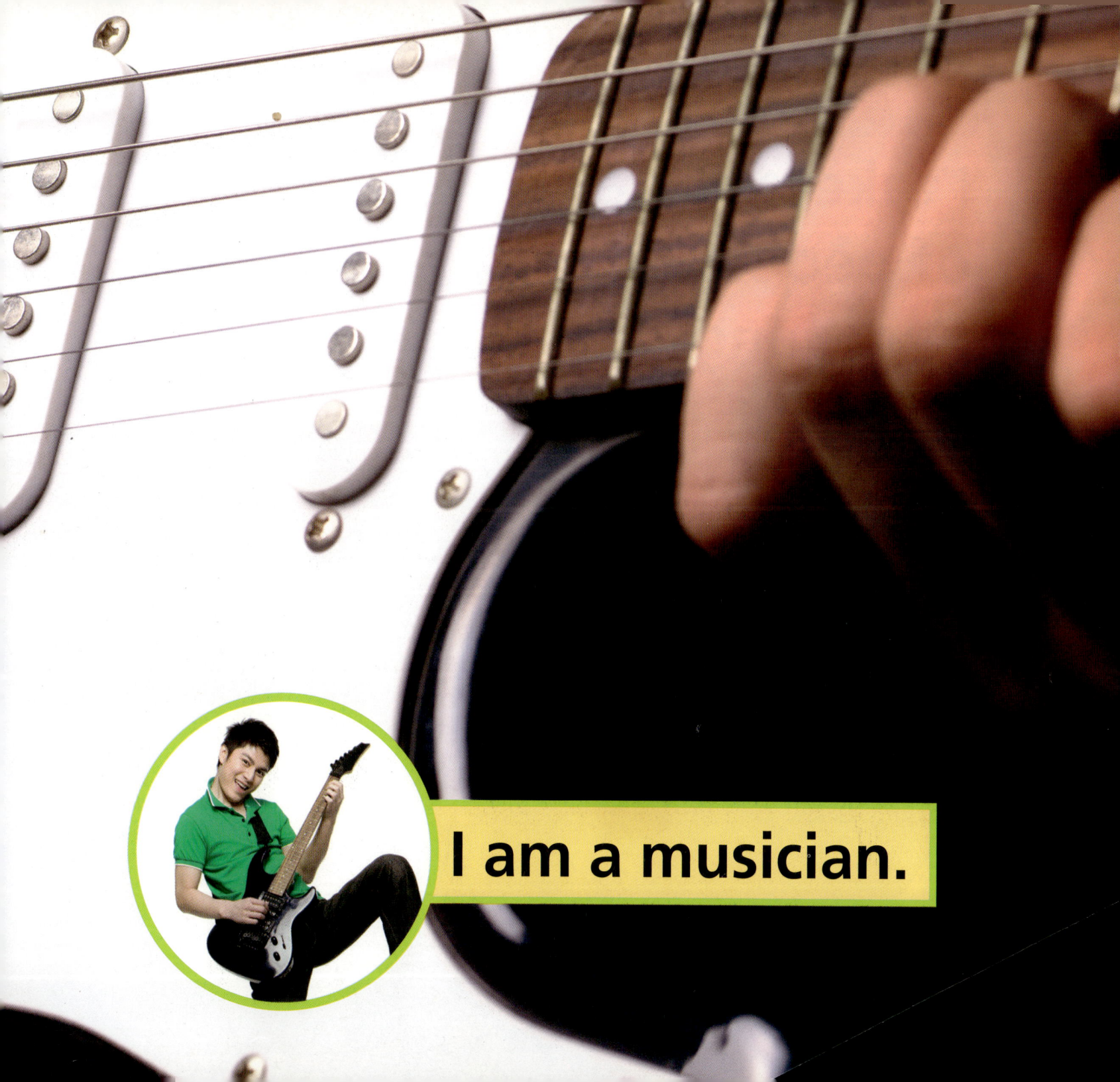

I am a musician.

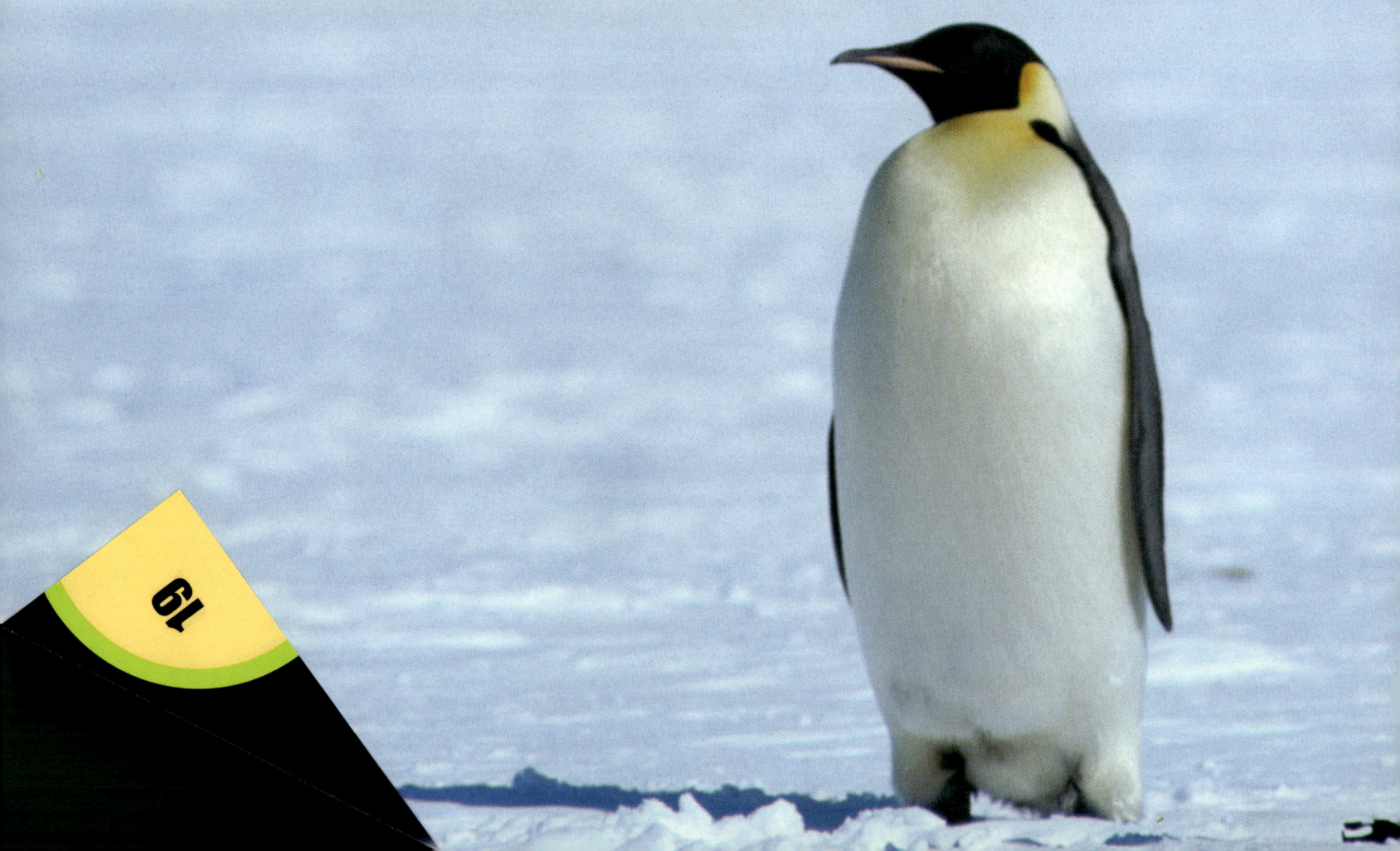

I take pictures of people, places, and things.

19

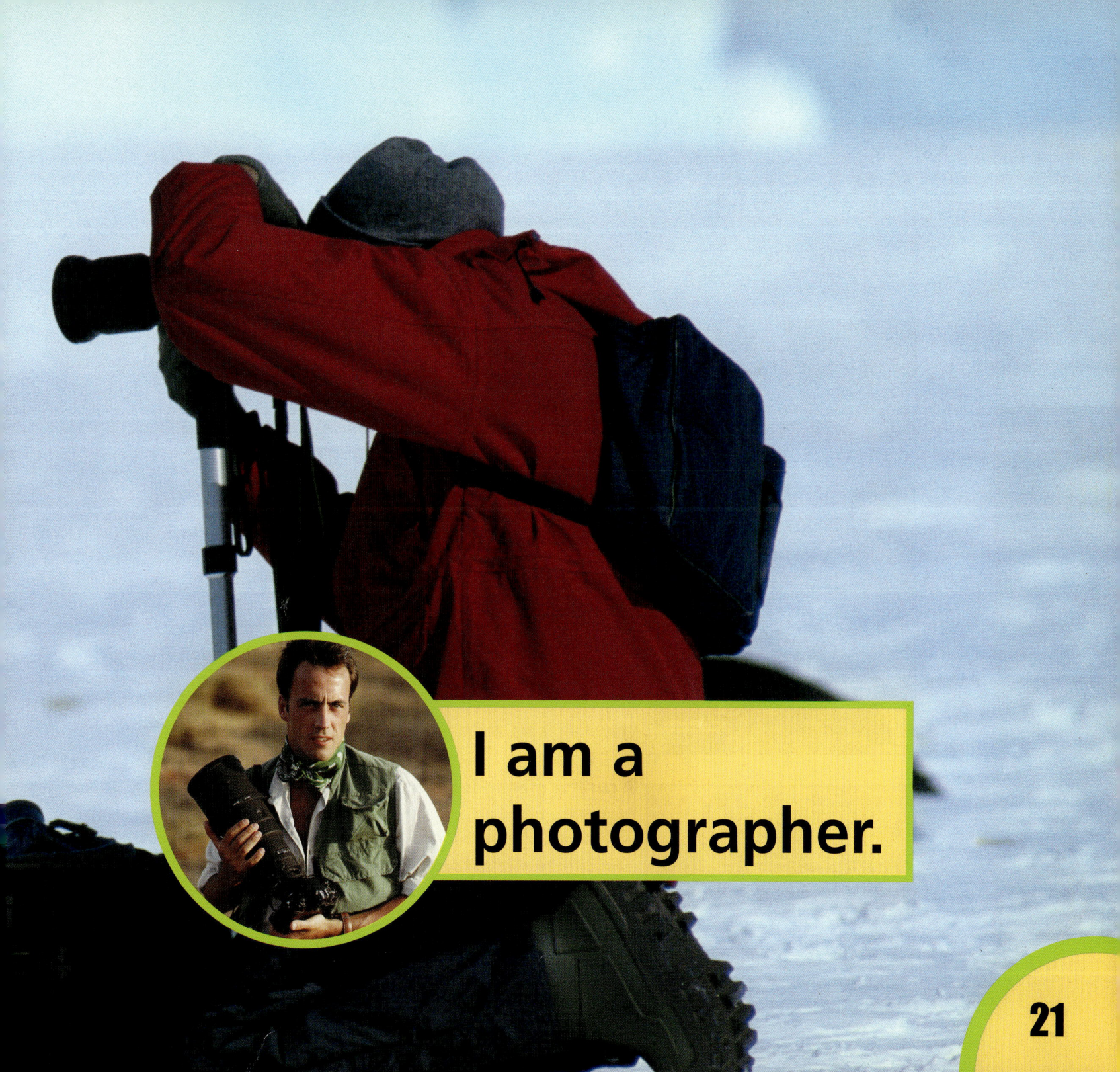

I am a photographer.

ARTS FACTS

People with common interests can form a community. The arts improve a community. They help people experience other points of view and learn about themselves and each other. Read more below about the careers of people involved in arts and culture.

Pages 4-5 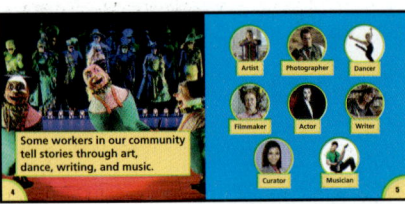 **The arts refer to visual, literary, and performing arts.** There are many professions in the arts, including working in art galleries and museums. Arts and cultural activities bring people in communities together.

Pages 6–7 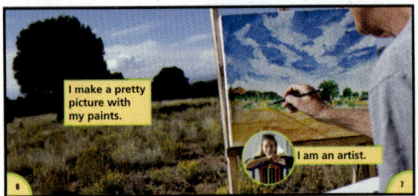 **Art can express what you are thinking and feeling.** Artists use many different methods and materials to make art. Paintings, drawings, sculptures, and creations done with a computer are some kinds of art. We may see art in public places, buildings, restaurants, and at home.

Pages 8–9 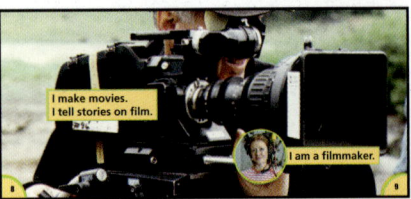 **Filmmakers make movies. They have many responsibilities.** They choose scripts, find funding for their films, assemble the cast, arrange filming locations, work with camera operators and other crew members, and try to keep filming on time and on budget.

Pages 10–11 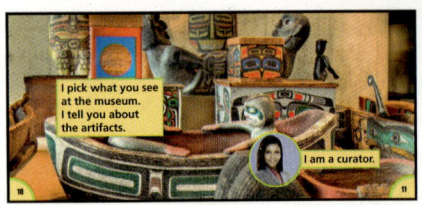 **A curator manages collections in a museum.** Curators usually have special training in archaeology, history, or anthropology. They work to acquire new items for the museum's collection and may travel the world to obtain them. Curators plan displays and conduct tours and museum programs. When we visit a museum, we learn about the history and art of a culture.

Pages 12–13 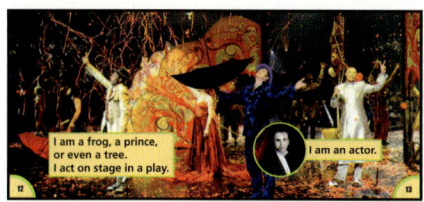 **Actors may work on stage, television shows, videos, movies, or radio programs.** They need many different talents and skills to do their job. These skills might include singing or dancing. Actors must also memorize lines from a script to play a part. They like to entertain people.

Pages 14–15 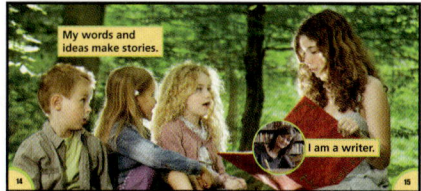 **There are many different kinds of writers.** Some make up stories from their imaginations. Newspaper and magazine writers write about things that really happen. Some writers may write as a career, and others may enjoy it as a hobby. Most writers are curious about the world and like to be creative with words.

Pages 16–17 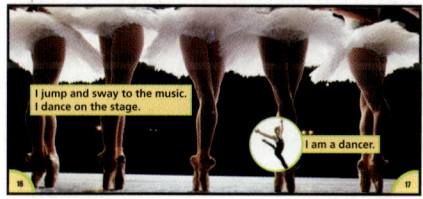 **Professional dancers spend many years training to be good enough to have a career in dance.** Most start training when they are children. Dancers may work onstage in theaters, at dance schools and studios, in movies, and at special events.

Pages 18–19 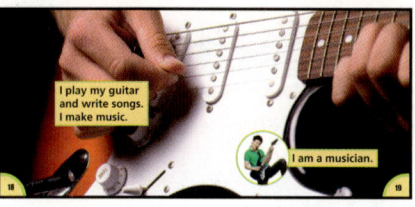 **Professional musicians may work alone or with a group of people in a band.** They must become experts at playing their instruments. Some also sing or write songs. They may perform onstage, or make music recorded onto other musicians' albums. Some musicians make the music we hear on TV and in movies and commercials.

Pages 20–21 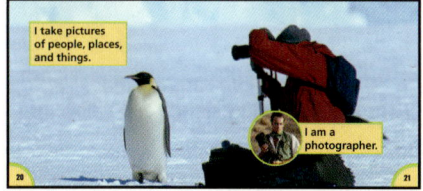 **Photographers work hard to get good pictures of people, places, and things.** They may work taking pictures of events such as weddings. Some take important pictures to go with news stories. Photographers also take pictures for books and magazines.

WORD LIST

Research has shown that as much as 65 percent of all written material published in English is made up of 300 words. These 300 words cannot be taught using pictures or learned by sounding them out. They must be recognized by sight. This book contains 34 common sight words to help young readers improve their reading fluency and comprehension. This book also teaches young readers several important content words, such as proper nouns. These words are paired with pictures to aid in learning and improve understanding.

Page	Sight Words First Appearance
4	and, in, our, some, tell, through
6	a, I, make, my, picture, with
7	an
8	on
10	about, at, see, the, what, you
12	even, or, play, tree
14	ideas, words
16	move, to
18	write
20	of, people, places, take, things

Page	Content Words First Appearance
4	art, community, dance, music, stories
5	actor, artist, curator, dancer, filmmaker, musician, photographer, writer
6	paints
8	film, movies
10	artifacts, museum
12	frog, prince, stage
16	music
18	guitar, songs

Check out av2books.com for activities, videos, audio clips, and more!

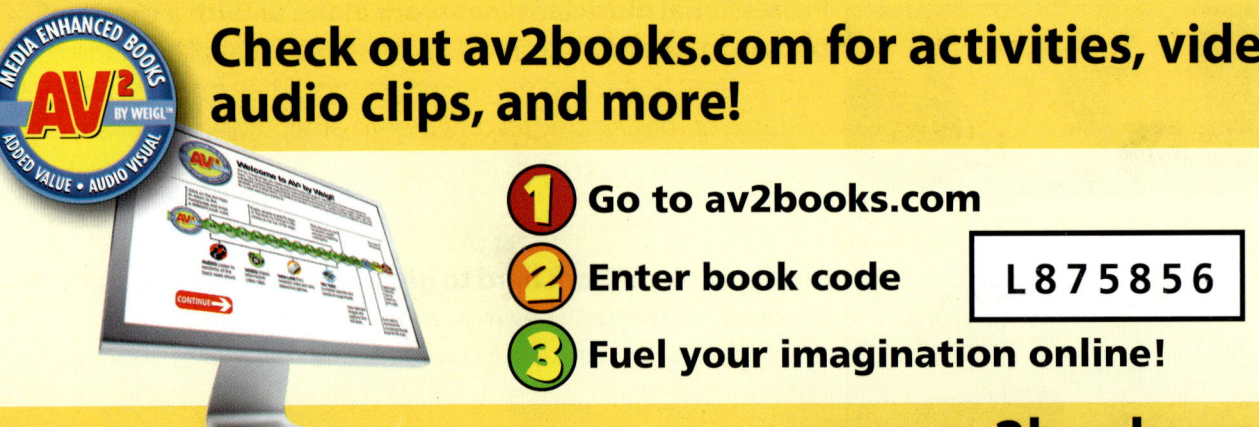

1. Go to av2books.com
2. Enter book code L 8 7 5 8 5 6
3. Fuel your imagination online!

www.av2books.com